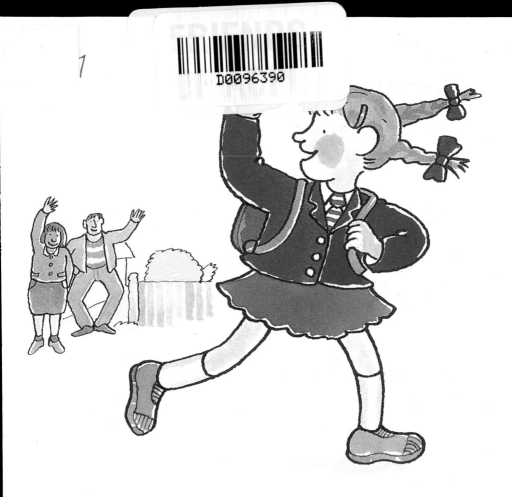

I went to school this morning
and I looked like this.

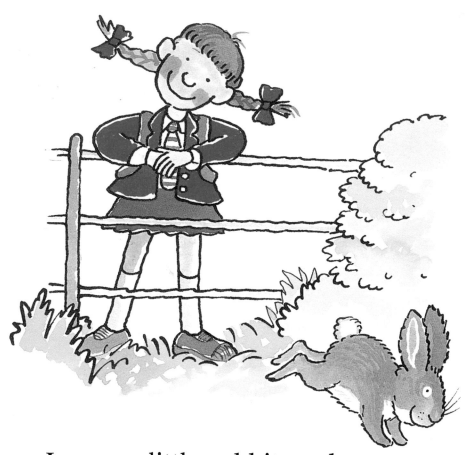

I saw a little rabbit and

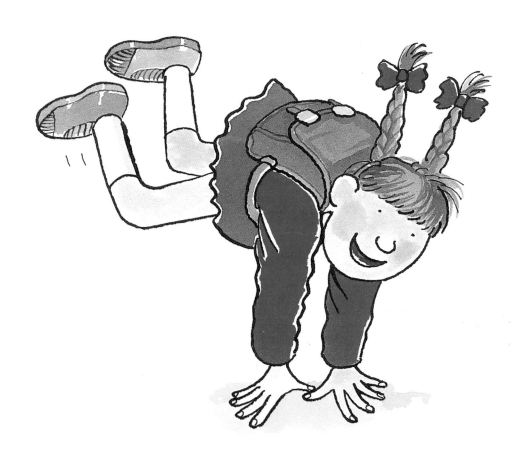

it hopped like this.

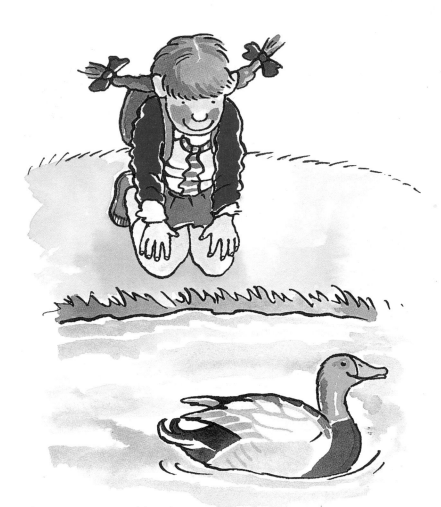

I saw a little duck and

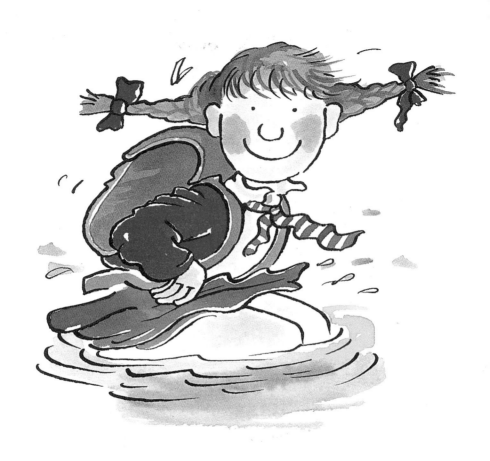

it swam like this.

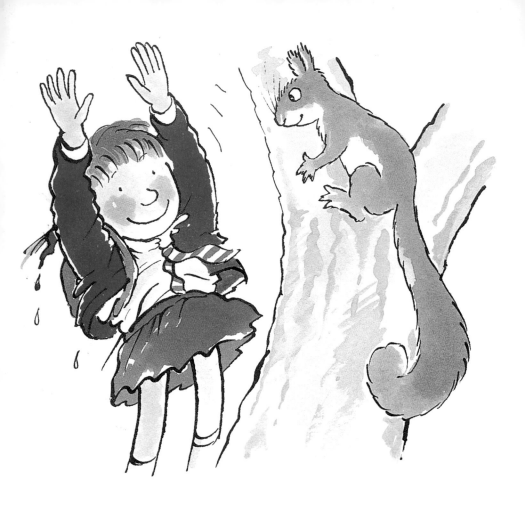

I saw a little squirrel and

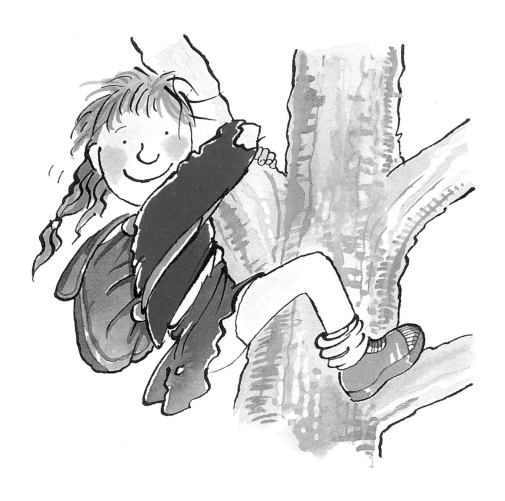

it climbed like this.

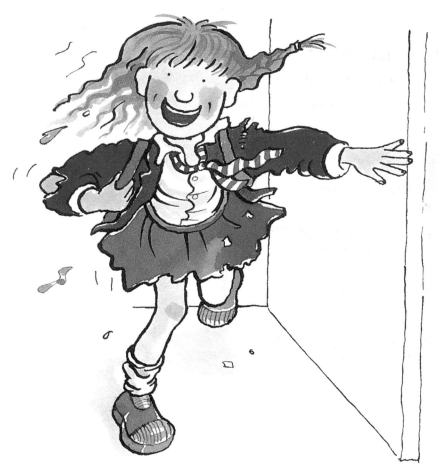

I went to school this morning
and I looked like this!